Beginner's
Cookbook

igloo

igloo

Published in 2007 by
Igloo Books Ltd
Cottage Farm,
Sywell,
NN6 0BJ
www.igloo-books.com

The publisher, author, and editor have made every
reasonable effort to ensure that the recipes in this book
are safe when made as instructed but assume no
responsibility for any damage caused or sustained while
making recipes in this book.

Some recipes in this book contain nuts.

ISBN: 978-1-84561-641-0

10 9 8 7 6 5 4 3 2 1

Project management: Toucan Books

Author: Jacqueline Bellefontaine
Design and layout: Bradbury and Williams
Cover image: © 2001 Rick Barrentine/Corbis
Editor: Theresa Bebbington
Interior photography: Cephas/Stockfood
Proofreader: Marion Dent
Printed in China

Contents

Get Cooking!

First read the advice on these pages to make sure you get the best results. After all, both you and your family will want to enjoy what they eat.

You will not only want to serve delicious meals, but also meals that are healthy and easy to make. It is important that growing children have a healthy balanced diet and the best way to get this balance is to feed your children a variety of foods. For this reason, we've often given variations with our recipes, but you can create your own.

Shopping for food
Buy the freshest food possible. Fresh fruit and vegetables are the healthiest option, especially organic ones, and frozen produce is better than tinned products. Always check the condition of the fruit and vegetables before you buy. Does the skin seem unmarked and taut? Avoid those that have too many blemishes (but a few blemishes are fine) or with wrinkled skin. When buying meat and fish, smell them before putting them in your shopping trolley. They should have a fresh smell - you'll soon learn when a smell indicates something that is a bit old.

For packaged products, make sure the packaging material isn't ripped or otherwise damaged, and don't buy tinned products that have dents in the tin, especially if the tin seems to be expanding - a sign of botulism that can be toxic.

The well-stocked kitchen
You'll soon discover which ingredients seem to be favorites because these will be the ones you run out of quickly. Always have some of the basic essentials in your cupboards. Examples include rice, pasta, sugar, flour (which may be better stored in the fridge), baking powder, bicarbonate of soda (baking soda), a vegetable oil, vinegar, a variety of sauces, and tinned tomatoes.

And don't forget the condiments. You'll want mayonnaise, ketchup, mustard, soy sauce, perhaps a meat tenderizer, and a variety of herbs and spices.

Measuring equipment
You can measure ingredients with a set of scales and weights or with a spring-type scale. The traditional scales with weights are

Basic kitchen equipment

Measuring equipment (see left)	Casserole dishes
Large and small chef's knives	Sieve
Serrated bread knife	Grater
2 chopping boards (reserve 1 for meat only)	Can opener
	Vegetable peeler
Oven gloves (mitts)	Wooden spoons
2 small, 1 medium, and 1 large saucepans	Fish slice or spatula
	Slotted spoon
Frying pan or skillet	Cooling rack
Small, medium, and large mixing bowls	
	Optional
Small heatproof bowl	Garlic press
Roasting pan	Lemon zester
Pie dish (pan)	Food processer
Baking tray	Handheld mixer or balloon whisk

the most accurate, and they now come with both metric and imperial measurements. Another way of measuring is to use measuring cups. These can be easier to use than fiddling about with scales. The recipes in this book use standard American measuring cups. You may need to visit a specialist kitchen shop to obtain some of the measuring equipment if items are not available in your area.

Always use professional-type measuring spoons, cups, and jugs – these are made to a standard size. A spoon from your kitchen drawer or a cup from the cupboard won't give you the correct measurements, and the recipes may not work. When using measuring cups and spoons, use the flat edge of a knife to level off the ingredients. Always stick to one system of measuring – never switch between metric and measuring cups.

Kitchen safety
Always read the recipe before you start and make sure you have all the ingredients and equipment you'll need ready. If you have long hair, tie it back, and keep ties and jewelry out of the way, too. Wash your hands before you start, and wash them again after handling meat.

Wash all fruit and vegetables before you use them. Always check the "use by" and "best before" dates – never use food that is out of date or with signs of mold. Always use a separate chopping board when cutting raw meat – never use it for fruit and vegetables.

Never put hot dishes directly on the work surface – use a trivet, mat, or wooden board to protect the surface. Always turn the handle of a saucepan on the hob (burner) to the side, where you are less likely to knock into it.

Breakfast in a Glass

Smoothies are a popular choice for breakfast. Try one of these three great smoothies, all of which will give you the energy to start your day.

 Serves 1-2
15 minutes

All-Year Berry Smoothie

Berries are packed with antioxidants. Buying them frozen is a good way to enjoy their benefits all year round.

115g/4oz/1 cup frozen mixed berries

225ml/8floz/1 cup yogurt

1 tbsp icing (confectioners') sugar

① Place all the ingredients in a blender and blend until smooth.

② If the smoothies are too thick, stir in a little milk to thin.

③ Pour into tall glasses to serve.

Easy Tropical Smoothie

These tropical fruits combine well with apple juice to be a welcoming, warm-weather treat.

1 wedge pineapple, peeled and cut into chunks

½ mango, peeled and cut into chunks

1 banana, cut into chunks

125ml/4floz/½ cup apple juice

① Reserve a piece of pineapple to decorate, then place all the ingredients in a blender and blend until smooth.

② Pour into a glass and decorate with the reserved pineapple to serve.

Strawberry Tofu Smoothie

This drink is a great energizer, perfect for a boost in the morning – or at any other time of the day.

225g/8oz/1 cup soft tofu

225g/8oz/2 cups strawberries, hulled

Splash orange juice, plus extra to dilute

1 tbsp sunflower seeds

① Place all the tofu, strawberries, and a splash of orange juice in a blender and blend until smooth.

② Add extra orange juice until you have a smoothie of your preferred thickness.

③ Pour into glasses and sprinkle with sunflower seeds.

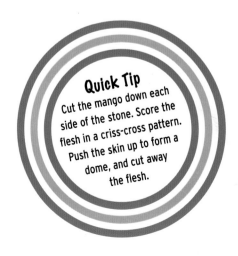

Quick Tip
Cut the mango down each side of the stone. Score the flesh in a criss-cross pattern. Push the skin up to form a dome, and cut away the flesh.

Variation Instead of blueberry sauce, top with **maple syrup** - you can also add a few **banana** slices to the pancakes after pouring the batter into the pan.

Pancakes

The blueberry sauce adds a delicious twist to these traditional pancakes, making them a real breakfast treat.

 Serves 2
15 minutes

Ingredients

115g/4oz/1 cup plain (all-purpose) flour

2 tbsp caster (superfine) sugar

1 tsp baking powder

150ml/5floz/⅔ cup buttermilk or low-fat natural (plain) yogurt

2 eggs

A little sunflower oil

100g/4oz/1 cup blueberries

4 tbsp orange juice

2 tbsp maple syrup

Smart Shopper

Buttermilk is an unusual ingredient. It is used for making pancakes because it adds flavor and texture, and it has less fat than whole-fat milk. If you forget to buy buttermilk, make a substitute by adding 1 tsp of lemon juice to 225ml/8floz/1 cup of milk, let sit for 5 minutes, then beat together. It will curdle, but don't worry – it's supposed to!

① Sift the flour into a bowl and stir in the sugar and baking powder. Add the buttermilk (or yogurt) and eggs and beat until smooth.

② To make the blueberry sauce, place the blueberries, orange juice, and maple syrup in a small pan and heat gently until the berries soften and their juice runs. Keep warm.

③ Heat a heavy-based frying pan or flat griddle pan and add a little oil. When the oil is hot, drop a large spoonful of the batter mixture into the pan and spread slightly.

④ Repeat with one or two more spoonfuls, depending on the size of the pan, to make several small pancakes.

⑤ Cook for about 2 minutes until golden on the underside and bubbles begin to appear on the surface. Flip over and cook for another 1 to 2 minutes.

⑥ Remove from the pan and keep warm. Repeat with the remaining mixture. Serve the pancakes with the blueberry sauce.

Quick Tip
To keep the pancakes warm until ready to serve, place on a heatproof plate, cover with foil, and keep in a warm oven.

Variation Add fried sliced **mushrooms** and chopped **parsley** after coating the base of the pan with the egg mixture and letting it set.

Easy Omelette

Omelettes are quick and easy to make. Make one at a time and serve immediately.

 Serves 1
15 minutes

Ingredients

2 eggs

1 tbsp milk

Salt and freshly ground black pepper

Pinch grated nutmeg

1 tsp sunflower oil

Small knob of butter

Smart Shopper

Basil, a good source of iron, calcium, and vitamin A, is used in many Italian dishes for flavoring and is one of the main ingredients in pesto. When possible, use fresh basil instead of dried basil because the fresh version has more flavor. Look for leaves that are dark green, without any spots or signs of yellowing.

① Break the eggs into a bowl and add the milk. Season with the salt, pepper, and nutmeg.

② Gently beat the eggs with a fork to combine the white, yolks, and milk.

③ Place a small frying pan over a medium heat and add the oil and butter. Once the butter has melted, swirl it around to coat the base of the pan.

④ Pour in the egg mixture and swirl the pan to coat the base. Allow the mixture to set for a few seconds, then using the side of the spoon, pull the edge of the omelette towards the centre and tilt the pan so that uncooked egg mixture runs to the side. Keep doing this until there is only a little liquid egg left.

⑤ Fold in half and slide the omelette onto a warm plate and serve.

Italian Omelette

Arrange 50g/2oz/½ cup sliced mozzarella cheese on top of the egg, then add 3 halved cherry tomatoes, followed by the basil. Place under a hot grill (broiler) for 1-2 minutes until the cheese begins to melt. Sprinkle with black pepper and a few fresh basil leaves. Slide onto a warm plate (without folding in half) and serve.

Quick Tip
If you don't have mozzarella cheese, you can use Cheddar cheese, Emmental (Swiss) cheese, or Monterey Jack cheese.

Variation Add a few leaves of your favorite **lettuce** to make a **BLT** - or bacon, lettuce, and tomato sandwich.

Bacon Sandwich

This winter warmer is ideal when you are about to confront an outdoors that is a little too cold for comfort.

 Serves 2
15 minutes

Ingredients

4 slices white, wholemeal (whole-wheat), or granary (whole-grain) bread

Butter or margarine for spreading

4 rashers (slices) bacon

1 ripe tomato, sliced

2 tbsp mayonnaise

Smart Shopper

Different types of bacon are sold in the supermarket. Look for one with more meat and less fat to make the best sandwich. Sometimes bacon is smoked to add hickory or oak flavor. Although smoked bacon is fine as a treat for adults, children might find that the flavoring is a little too strong for their tastes.

① Toast the bread if desired. Spread the bread with a little butter or margarine.

② Grill (broil) or fry the bacon, turning once, for 3-5 minutes. Or grill or fry it for a little longer if you prefer your bacon crispy.

③ Place two rashers (slices) of bacon on each of two slices of bread, then add the tomato slices and a dab of mayonnaise.

④ Place the remaining bread slices on top, cut in half, and serve.

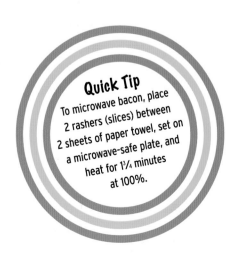

Quick Tip
To microwave bacon, place 2 rashers (slices) between 2 sheets of paper towel, set on a microwave-safe plate, and heat for 1¾ minutes at 100%.

Muffin Master

These not-too-sweet cakes are best served warm on the day they are made. They make a great breakfast treat.

 Makes 12
30 minutes

Ingredients
Basic Recipe:
400g/14oz/3½ cups plain (all-purpose) flour

1 tsp bicarbonate of soda (baking soda)

1 tsp ground cinnamon

175g/6oz/¾ cup caster (superfine) sugar

3 eggs

300ml/10floz/1¼ cup buttermilk

3 tbsp butter, melted

Smart Shopper
A very fine type of sugar was named caster sugar (also known as superfine sugar) because the grains are small enough to fit through a sugar caster, or sugar sprinkler. It dissolves more quickly than regular sugar, making it ideal for baking. You can make your own caster sugar by grinding regular granulated sugar in a food processor.

① Line 12 muffin tins with paper cases. Preheat the oven to 190°C/375°F/gas mark 5.

② Place the flour, bicarbonate of soda (baking soda), cinnamon, and sugar in a large mixing bowl and stir to mix well.

③ Beat together the eggs and buttermilk until well combined. Stir into the flour mixture until just blended. Drizzle over the melted butter and stir in.

④ Divide the mixture between the paper muffin cases, filling almost to the top. Bake for 30-35 minutes until a skewer inserted into the centre comes out clean. Let the muffins cool in the tin for 5 minutes.

Blueberry Muffins
Follow the recipe; fold in 250g/9oz/2 cups blueberries with the butter.

Banana Muffins
Mash 1 large ripe banana with a fork and beat into the egg mixture.

Chocolate Muffins
Melt 85g/3oz plain (dark) chocolate in a bowl over a pan of simmering water. Follow the recipe, omitting the cinnamon. Fold in the melted chocolate and 50g/2oz chocolate chips with the butter.

Quick Tip
You won't need to beat the muffin mixture for too long. A few lumps are better than over-beating, which makes the muffins tough.

Simple Fruit Salad

You can prepare this fruit salad the night before so you won't have the fuss of preparing it at breakfast time.

 Serves 4
20 minutes

Ingredients

3 oranges

2 red apples

2 kiwi fruits

2 bananas

225ml/8floz/1 cup orange juice

1-2 tbsp clear honey (optional)

Smart Shopper

Before purchasing fruit you should make sure it is ripe. Don't buy oranges that have signs of mold. A pineapple should have a fragrant odor and green leaves. Avoid pineapples with brown spots. A ripe mango gives slightly when pressed and has an orange or reddish skin. Don't buy a mango with dark spots – the flesh is bruised.

① Peel and segment the oranges. To do this without any pith, cut the top and bottom off the oranges. Using a sharp knife, cut the peel away from the oranges in downwards strips. Remove the segments by sliding the knife between the membranes. Place the segments in a serving bowl.

② Remove the core from the apples and cut the fruit into thin wedges. Peel and slice the kiwi fruits, then cut the slices in half. Peel and slice the bananas. Add the fruit to the bowl.

③ Pour the orange juice over the fruit and sweeten with honey if desired.

④ Toss the fruit until well combined and chill until ready to serve.

✖ Tropical Fruit Salad

Instead of the oranges, add the chunks of 1 mango (see *Quick Tip*, page 7) and chunks of ½ a pineapple (see *Quick Tip*, right) to the bowl. Cut 1 papaya in half, scoop out the seeds, peel, cut the flesh into chunks, and add to the bowl. Instead of the pineapple juice, use 300ml/10floz/1¼ cups of orange juice, and add a 5cm/2 inch piece of peeled and grated ginger with the honey.

Quick Tip
To cut up a pineapple, start by cutting it into wedges, then cut away the peel and tough centre core. Now cut the flesh into chunks.

The Best Lunchboxes

Variety is the spice of life and that includes lunchtime and the lunchbox. Plan a different lunch for every day.

Variety is also the key to a healthy, balanced diet. Although okay sometimes, don't pack the same old sandwich, packet of crisps (potato chips), and piece of fruit every day. Besides not providing children with the variety they need, it also becomes dull and may well arrive back at home uneaten.

It is important that children eat lunch so their concentration levels are maintained during the afternoon. There is evidence that what your children eat affects their behavior after a meal, so it has never been more important to ensure you pack a good lunchbox. Minerals and vitamins found in fruit and vegetables will provide vital elements for good health and will help your children do to their best at school.

Bite-size foods

Instead of sandwiches, why not give a younger child a selection of bite-size foods to nibble on. Cubes of cheese, slices of ham, mini sausages, hard boiled eggs, sticks of carrot and celery, and cherry tomatoes can be packed into small containers. You can also supply small containers of dips such as hummus to serve with the vegetable sticks, along with a few corn chips to create a nutritious, balanced meal.

Pasta salad

Add some variety by packing a pasta salad in the lunchbox. You can make a simple one by mixing cooked pasta with cubes of cheese or ham, diced pepper, and halved cherry tomatoes, then tossing in a little mayonnaise.

Rice salad

Another type of salad that is sure to please is a rice salad. Mix cooked rice (see pages 70-71) with diced peppers and cucumber, and with cooked peas and diced carrots (let the cooked vegetables cool down before adding them to the salad). Toss in a little vinaigrette dressing.

Bread and cake

Remember your child needs a lot of energy to keep going through the day, so include some carbohydrates. This may be bread, but it can also be supplied as a muffin (see pages 14-15), piece of cake, or a biscuit (cookie) - as long as it isn't too sweet.

Fruit

Include some fruit for vital nutrients. This may be a single piece of fruit or a mini fruit salad. Dried fruits such as apricots, prunes, apple slices, and raisins are good to include for healthy nibbles.

Or make your own fruit yogurt - it will have much less sugar than those bought from the shops. Stir chopped fruit into natural (plain) yogurt and sweeten with a little honey. If your child doesn't like chunks, purée soft fruits such as strawberries, blueberries, or raspberries in a blender and stir into the yogurt.

Quick Tip
Don't forget to include a drink in the lunchbox. Water is best, but you can also pack diluted fruit juice as a healthy option.

Variation Replace the lettuce leaves with other healthy green options such as **spinach** or **rocket** (arugula).

Chicken Club Sandwich

These hearty sandwiches are ideal for the lunchbox, but if eating at home, you can also add slices of tomato.

Serves 2
15 minutes

Ingredients

4 rashers (slices) bacon

6 thin slices of crusty bread

Mayonnaise

175g/6oz cooked chicken, sliced

2 tbsp mayonnaise (optional)

Few salad leaves or watercress

1 tomato, sliced

Smart Shopper

The peppery dark green leaves of watercress are among the most nutritious salad greens. When buying watercress, look for crisp, bright green leaves, avoiding those that are wilted or yellow. If the flavor is too strong for your children, use the milder lettuce leaves instead.

① Grill or fry the bacon until crispy.

① Toast the bread if desired. Spread two slices of bread with a little mayonnaise.

② Top two slices of bread with the chicken, then with mayonnaise and some lettuce leaves or watercress.

③ Place a slice of bread on top of the chicken and spread with a little mayonnaise.

④ Place the bacon and tomato on the bread and sandwich together with the remaining bread.

⑤ Cut the two sandwiches in half or quarters and serve.

Quick Tip
If you use thicker bread, make each sandwich with only 2 slices of bread, omitting the middle slice of bread.

Variation Add some chopped **black olives** instead of the celery and onion and top with a slice of **avocado** after melting the cheese.

Tuna Melt

This is a quick, nutritious lunch that can be made in minutes.

 Serves 2
15 minutes

Ingredients

200g/7oz can tuna, drained

6 spring onions (scallions), sliced

1 stick celery, thinly sliced

½ red pepper, diced

6 tbsp mayonnaise

4 slices bread

Few leaves of lettuce (optional)

2 slices of cheese

Smart Shopper

Get cheesy by choosing the right cheese to go with the tuna melt. Kids often object to strong flavors, so use a mild cheese to make this one a hit with your kids. For a more adult taste, try a strong aged cheddar. A little will go a long way, so you can get a great cheese taste with a smaller quantity of strong cheese, which cuts down on fat.

1. Mix together the tuna, onions, celery, pepper, and mayonnaise until well combined.

2. Lightly toast the bread under a hot grill (broiler).

3. Place the lettuce, if using, on two slices of toast, and divide the tuna mixture between the two.

4. Place a slice of cheese on top and return to the grill (broiler). Heat until the cheese melts.

5. Top with the remaining toast, then cut in half and serve.

Quick Tip
To avoid a runny mixture, squeeze all the liquid from the tuna. After opening the can, push down on the lid, avoiding the sharp edges.

Hearty Salad

Make up a home salad bar and let the family pick and choose their favorite combination.

 Serves 2
30 minutes

Group 1

Salad leaves

Cucumber, sliced

Cherry tomatoes

Cooked beetroot (beet), sliced or diced

Carrot, grated

Radish, sliced

Sweet corn niblets (corn kernels)

Celery sticks

Red or yellow peppers, sliced

Mushrooms, sliced

Group 2

Hard boiled eggs

Sliced ham

Sliced chicken

Pastrami

Cheese

Tuna

Salami

Quick Tip

Salad leaves such as lettuce are better in salads torn instead of chopped. Provide a few types of lettuce for variety in texture.

Each diner should choose 4 to 6 items from group 1 and 2 or 3 items from group 2, place them in a bowl, then top with a little of their favorite dressing.

Salad Dressings

French Dressing:

6 tbsp olive oil

2 tbsp white wine vinegar

Salt and freshly ground black pepper

Whisk the ingredients together.

Yogurt Dressing:

125ml/4floz/½ cup natural (plain) yogurt

1 garlic clove, crushed

2 tbsp lemon juice

Salt and freshly ground black pepper

Stir the ingredients together.

Light Mayonnaise Dressing:

6 tbsp mayonnaise

3 tbsp natural (plain) yogurt

1 tbsp chives, snipped

Mix the ingredients together until smooth.

Blue Cheese Dressing:

50g/2oz/½ cup blue cheese, mashed with a fork

3 tbsp mayonnaise

3 tbsp double (heavy) cream

Freshly ground black pepper

Mix the ingredients together until smooth.

Variation Try topping the filling with a little grated **Monterey Jack cheese.**

Chicken Fajitas

This Mexican favorite is easy to cook and assemble and should be a hit with the kids.

Serves 2
20 minutes, plus marinating time

Ingredients

2 skinned and boned chicken breasts, about 175g/6oz each

Juice of 2 limes

2 tbsp freshly chopped coriander (cilantro)

2 tbsp sunflower oil

½ tsp chilli flakes

¼ tsp ground coriander

1 each red and green pepper, seeded and cut into strips

1 onion, sliced

8 Mexican flour tortillas

Guacamole, tomato salsa, and soured cream

Smart Shopper

Tortillas are flat unleavened bread made from maize (corn) or wheat flour. Corn tortillas have a stronger flavor that is more suitable for beef-based dishes.

Besides using tortillas for Mexican meals, use them wrapped around traditional sandwich fillers such as ham, cheese, and tomato, with a sprinkling of salad dressing.

① Cut the chicken breasts into thin strips and place in a shallow non-metallic dish.

② Combine the lime juice, fresh coriander (cilantro), 1 tbsp oil, chilli, and ground coriander, and pour over the meat. Toss to combine and allow to marinate for at least 30 minutes in the refrigerator.

③ Heat the remaining oil in a frying pan. Remove the chicken from the marinade and add to the pan. Fry over a high heat for about 5 minutes until well browned on all sides.

④ Add the peppers and onion, and fry for 5 minutes until softened. Pour in any remaining marinade and fry for 1 minute.

⑤ Meanwhile, warm the tortillas as directed on the packet.

⑥ Serve filled with the meat mixture, and include a spoonful each of the salsa, guacamole, and soured cream on the side.

Quick Tip
If the chicken breasts still have skin, simply peel it away with your fingers. It's easy to remove flesh from the bone with a sharp knife.

Jacket Potatoes

This versatile dish can be served with butter as a side dish for a main meal or with a choice of fillings for lunch.

 Serves 4
1 hour 20 minutes

Ingredients
4 baking potatoes, about 300g/10oz each
Filling of your choice (see below) or butter to serve

Smart Shopper
Not all potatoes are suitable as baking potatoes. Those used for baking are low in moisture and have dry fluffy flesh when cooked. Choose potatoes that are firm with tight skin. Avoid those that have dark spots, cuts, or cracks, and also if they have any signs of green – these will be bitter and can even be poisonous.

① Preheat the oven to 200°C/400°F/gas mark 6. Scrub the potatoes well and prick all over with a fork (to prevent them from exploding in the oven).

② Place on a baking sheet and bake in the hottest part of the oven for 1¼ hours, turning once.

③ When cooked, cut a large cross into the potatoes and squeeze to open out.

④ Place on a serving plate and served topped with a generous wedge of butter or a filling of your choice.

Fillings:

☒ **Baked Beans:** Pour a 400g/14oz can baked beans into a small saucepan and heat gently, stirring, for 4-5 minutes until piping hot.

☒ **Cheese:** Coarsely grate 175g/6oz/1½ cups of cheese and divide between the 4 potatoes.

☒ **Coleslaw:** Allow 50g/2oz/⅓ cup of coleslaw per person.

☒ **Peanut Butter:** Top the potatoes with 2 tbsp of smooth or crunchy peanut butter in place of butter.

☒ **Tuna Mayo:** Mix a 200g/7oz can tuna, drained, with 4 tbsp mayonnaise and 2 tbsp sweet corn niblets (corn kernels).

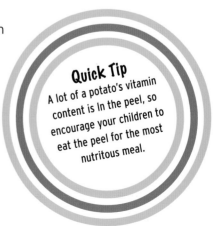
Quick Tip
A lot of a potato's vitamin content is in the peel, so encourage your children to eat the peel for the most nutritous meal.

Variation You can add 250g/9oz/2 cups peeled and cubed **squash** or a peeled and chopped **sweet potato** with the leek and carrot.

Easy Vegetable Soup

The combination of vegetables makes this a nutritious lunch, and it is also easy to prepare.

Serves 4
45 minutes

Ingredients

2 tbsp olive oil

1 leek, sliced

1 clove garlic, chopped

1 carrot, diced

400g/14oz can chopped tomatoes

900ml/30floz/4 cups vegetable stock

1 courgette (zucchini), diced

1 red pepper, seeded and diced

50g/2oz short-cut macaroni

Salt and freshly ground black pepper

4 tsp pesto or basil leaves to garnish

Grated fresh Parmesan cheese to sprinkle

Smart Shopper

You can use a store-bought vegetable stock but they are not as good as homemade. To make your own, simmer 1 sliced onion, leek, carrot, and parsnip, plus 6 cloves of crushed garlic, with 1400ml/48floz/6 cups of water and some dried herbs of your choice for 45 to 60 minutes. Strain the stock through a sieve.

① Heat the oil in a large saucepan, add the leek and carrot, and gently fry for 5 minutes until the vegetables begin to soften. Do not let them burn.

② Stir in the garlic and fry for 1 minute.

③ Stir in the tomatoes and stock, and bring to the boil. Simmer for 20 minutes.

④ Add the courgette (zucchini), red pepper, and macaroni, and simmer for 10 minutes. Season with salt and pepper.

⑤ Serve in warm bowls with a spoonful of pesto or a few basil leaves and sprinkle with Parmasan cheese.

Quick Tip

Trimming the ends of the clove of garlic with a sharp knife will make it easier to remove the skin before you chop the garlic.

Variation You can add some freshly grated **Parmesan cheese** if you like. Sprinkle it over the butter.

Garlic Bread

This is a great accompaniment to soup, salad, and pasta, all of which are ideal for lunch.

 Serves 4
30 minutes

2 cloves garlic, crushed
1 tbsp freshly chopped parsley
115g/4oz/1 stick butter, softened
1 loaf French bread

Smart Shopper

Fresh crusty bread is the most important ingredient in this recipe. If you can't find fresh French bread, then try a different type of crusty bread or even rolls. Bread from the supermarket may contain preservatives, so try purchasing bread from a local bakery.

1. Preheat the oven to 180°C/350°F/gas mark 4.
2. Place the garlic, parsley, and butter in a mixing bowl, and beat with a wooden spoon until well combined.
3. Cut the bread into 2.5-cm/1-inch thick slices.
4. Spread each slice with the seasoned butter and reassemble the loaf.
5. Wrap the loaf well in foil. It may be easier to do this in two parcels.
6. Bake for 20 minutes. Serve while still hot.

Quick Tip

Cut the bread all the way through so you can separate the hot slices easily when served, but reassemble in a loaf shape before you bake it.

Variation For an interesting change, try adding a little diced **red pepper**.

Guacamole with Chips

This makes a nice snack on its own, or serve with Chicken Fajitas (see pages 26-27) to make a Mexican dinner.

Serves 4
30 minutes

Ingredients

2 ripe avocados

2 tbsp lemon juice

2 tomatoes

½ small onion, finely chopped

1 clove garlic, crushed

½ tsp ground cumin

½ tsp ground coriander

2 tbsp freshly chopped coriander (cilantro)

Pinch sugar, salt, and freshly ground black pepper

Corn chips to serve

Smart Shopper

Avocados have a bitter taste if cooked, so always use them raw. To tell if an avocado is ripe, squeeze it gently. It should feel tender. If you buy an unripe avocado, it should mature within about 3 days. You can put one in a brown paper bag with an apple to speed up the ripening process. Overripe avocados are only good for using mashed.

1. Cut the avocados in half and remove the stone by tapping sharply with the blade of a sharp knife so that it goes into the stone. Twist the knife to remove the stone.

2. Scoop out the flesh into a bowl. Add the lemon juice and mash coarsely with a fork.

3. Skin the tomatoes if desired. Cut in half, then scoop out and discard the seeds. Chop the flesh.

4. Add the tomato, onion, garlic, ground cumin and coriander, and chopped coriander (cilantro) to the bowl, and beat to combine.

5. Season with the sugar, salt, and pepper.

6. Transfer to a serving dish and serve with the corn chips.

Quick Tip
To peel a tomato, put it in boiling water for 1 minute, then cold water for 1 minute. Cut into the skin with a knife, then use fingers to peel it off.

Variation Instead of lettuce on one half of a bun, replace with a slice of your favorite **cheese** and melt under the grill (broiler) for a minute or so.

Hamburgers

Named after Hamburg in Germany, hamburgers are made with beef. Tasty homemade burgers are easy to make.

 Serves 4
30 minutes

Ingredients

700g/1lb8oz minced (ground) beef

Salt and freshly ground black pepper

1 tsp chilli powder or dried mixed herbs

4 burger buns

Handful of salad leaves

2 tomatoes, sliced

Sliced pickles

Smart Shopper

When choosing your minced (ground) beef, look for meat that has some fat to help the cooking process but not so much fat (the meat will have a pale pink color) that it all shrinks away. Look for pale red or pink meat; red means additives. Untreated beef naturally darkens when exposed to light – this is fine. Make sure it has a fresh smell.

① Place the beef in a large mixing bowl and season well with salt and pepper. Sprinkle the chilli powder or herbs over the meat, and using your fingers, mix until well combined.

② Press the meat together and shape into 4 burgers, no more than 2.5cm/1 inch thick. Cook the burgers under a medium-hot grill for 5–6 minutes each side or until cooked through.

③ Cut the burger buns in half and lightly toast if desired. Place one half on each serving plate and place a few salad leaves on each. Place a burger on the salad leaves and top with sliced tomatoes and pickles.

④ Place the burger bun on top and serve immediately.

Quick Tip

To shape a burger "patty", form a ball of the meat. Press the ball between the palm of your hands and rotate it to form an even round circle.

Variation Replace the carrots with 1-2 **sweet potatoes** or a **squash**, peeled and cubed.

Lamb Casserole

Prunes add a Moroccan touch to this recipe. Children often enjoy the sweetness that it adds to the dish, making this easy casserole a favorite.

 Serves 4
2 hours

Ingredients

2 tbsp flour

½ tsp ground coriander

¼ tsp ground cinnamon

Salt and freshly ground black pepper

700g/1lb8oz lean lamb, cubed

2 tbsp olive oil

1 large onion, sliced

3 medium potatoes, peeled and cut into large chunks

6 large carrots, peeled and thickly sliced

1 litre/34floz/4¼ cups lamb or vegetable stock

115g/4oz/½ cup prunes, stoned

Smart Shopper

Lamb sold for stews and casseroles come from several parts of the animal. Look for cuts from the shoulder, which will be tender and have the best flavor, and – unlike cuts from the leg – they won't dry out. Lamb from the neck is also flavorful and suitable for stews, but it will be less meaty than other cuts.

① Combine the flour, spices, salt, and pepper in a bag. Add the meat and shake until the meat is coated in the flour mixture.

② Heat the oil in a large flameproof casserole and quickly brown the meat in batches. If you try browning all the meat at once, there will be too much meat in the pan and it will steam instead of fry.

③ Return all the meat to the pan. Stir in the vegetables and add any remaining flour from the bag.

④ Stir in the stock and bring to the boil. Cover and simmer gently for 1 hour. Add the prunes and cook for 30 minutes, stirring occasionally.

⑤ Serve as a meal on its own with rice or serve with fresh cooked green vegetables.

Quick Tip
When browning the meat, make sure all the edges change color – this seals in the juice for tender meat and also helps it to cook fully.

Variation For a change of pace, bake chicken wings in this barbeque sauce instead of the spare ribs.

Sticky Spare Ribs

Remember to have plenty of napkins handy for wiping sticky fingers clean.

 Serves 4
60 minutes

Ingredients

1.4kg/3lb pork ribs

3 tbsp honey

3 tbsp tomato ketchup

4 tbsp brown sauce or meat tenderizer sauce

2 tbsp dry sherry

1 clove garlic, crushed

1 tbsp grated root ginger

1 tbsp dry wholegrain mustard

1 tbsp sweet chilli sauce

Smart Shopper

There are different types of pork ribs. The ribs that have the least amount of meat are the ones that many people consider to be the most tasty. Other types of ribs are more meaty and have less fat – but to gain these benefits you'll have to be willing to give up some of the flavor.

① Preheat the oven to 190°C/375°F/gas mark 5.

② Bring a large pan of water to the boil and add the ribs. Return to the boil, reduce the heat, and simmer for 20 minutes. Drain and let cool slightly.

③ Combine the honey, tomato ketchup, brown sauce, sherry, garlic, ginger, mustard, and chilli sauce in a large shallow dish. Add the ribs and toss in the mixture until well coated.

④ Arrange in a single layer on a baking sheet and bake for 25 minutes in the preheated oven. Alternatively, cook under a hot grill (broiler) or on a barbeque for about 25 minutes, turning frequently.

⑤ Let cool for 5 minutes before serving.

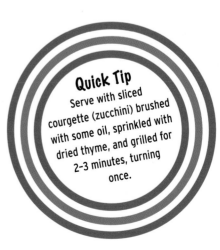

Quick Tip
Serve with sliced courgette (zucchini) brushed with some oil, sprinkled with dried thyme, and grilled for 2-3 minutes, turning once.

Lamb with Gremolata

Allow 2 to 3 cutlets per adult and 1 to 2 cutlets per child. Gremolata is an Italian accompaniment often used for veal.

Serves 4
30 minutes

Ingredients

8 lamb cutlets, trimmed

2 tbsp lemon juice

1 tbsp olive oil

1 clove garlic, crushed

Gremolata:

1 clove garlic, peeled and finely chopped

Zest of 1 lemon

2 tbsp freshly chopped parsley

Smart Shopper

There are different lamb cutlets available. Look for the leanest cuts with creamy white fat. If the fat looks brittle and yellowish instead of firm, the meat is old and should be avoided. The color of the meat varies, according to where the lamb was raised. If you don't know how to trim the lamb, ask a butcher to do it for you.

1. Preheat the grill (broiler) to a high setting.

2. Mix the lemon juice, oil, and garlic, and brush the mixture over the cutlets.

3. Cook under the grill (broiler) for 3–6 minutes each side, depending on how well done you like the lamb to be cooked. Brush with any remaining baste as the cutlets cook.

4. Meanwhile, combine the finely chopped garlic, lemon zest, and parsley in a small bowl to make the gremolata.

5. Serve the lamb cutlets with a little of the gremolata spooned on top. You can also serve with grilled tomatoes and a crisp green salad if you desire.

Quick Tip
The zest is the outermost part of the peel. Use a lemon zester to remove fine strands of zest, or finely grate it if you don't have a zester.

Variation For a vegetarian pie, add 175g/6oz/1¾ cups each of blanched **broccoli** and **cauliflower** and 50g/2oz/⅓ cup **peas** to the sauce in step 2 instead of adding the chicken.

Chicken Pot Pie

You can make one large or several individual pies - you'll need the larger quantity of pastry if making small pies.

 Serves 4
1 hour 20 minutes

Ingredients

2 tbsp butter

2 leeks, washed, trimmed, and sliced

2 carrots, washed, trimmed, and sliced

50g/2oz/½ cup plain (all-purpose) flour

300ml/10floz/1¼ cups chicken stock

150ml/5floz/⅔ cup milk

450g/1lb cooked chicken

1 tbsp freshly chopped parsley

Salt and freshly ground black pepper

225g-350g/8-12oz puff or shortcrust pastry, thawed if frozen

1 egg, beaten, to glaze

Smart Shopper

If you can't make your own pastry, you can buy it already made at a supermarket. There are different types available. Puff pastry is rolled and folded in layers to make a light fluffy pastry. Shortcrust pastry is not as flaky as puff pastry. It's often used as a pie base.

① Preheat the oven to 200°C/400°F/gas mark 6. Melt the butter in a small pan and fry the leeks and carrots for about 5 minutes until softened.

② Stir in the flour and cook for a few seconds. Gradually stir in the stock and milk, and cook gently, stirring, until the sauce thickens. Add the chicken and parsley. Season with salt and pepper. Pour into a pie dish (pie pan).

③ Roll out the pastry a little larger than the pie dish and cut a strip of pastry from the edge. Dampen the edge of the pie dish with a little beaten egg and stick the pastry strip in place around the rim.

④ Dampen the pastry strip and place the pastry on top. Press the edges down with a fork to seal together. Cut a small slit in the pastry to allow the steam to escape, and decorate with pastry trimmings cut into shapes if desired. Brush the pastry with a little beaten egg.

⑤ Bake for 20 minutes, then reduce the heat to 180°C/350°F/gas mark 4 and bake for a further 20 minutes until the pastry is crisp and golden.

Quick Tip
If you want to add the broccoli and cauliflower, put them in boiling water for 4 minutes to blanch them before adding to the sauce.

Chicken Curry

This is a creamy mild-flavoured Indian dish that all the family will love.

  Serves 4
60 minutes

Ingredients

2 tbsp sunflower oil

700g/1lb8oz chicken meat, cut into cubes

2 small onions, cut into wedges

2 sticks celery, sliced

1 clove garlic, crushed

1 tbsp mild curry paste

½ tsp ground turmeric

50g/2oz/⅓ cup creamed coconut

225ml/8floz/1 cup chicken stock

125ml/4floz/½ cup natural yogurt

Smart Shopper

Turmeric should be found in the herb and spice section of your supermarket. For curry paste and creamed coconut, look in the ethnic section. The creamed coconut comes in a block and you shave off what you need. If it's not available in your area, substitute with coconut milk.

① Heat the oil in a saucepan and fry the chicken until browned on all sides. Remove from the pan.

② Add the onions and celery and cook for 3 minutes. Then stir in the garlic, curry paste, and turmeric, and cook gently for 2 minutes. Add the coconut and stir until melted.

③ Add the stock and bring to the boil. Return the chicken to the pan. Reduce the heat and simmer covered for 30 minutes.

④ Stir in the yogurt and serve with rice (see pages 70-71) and a vegetable such as peas. Garnish with parsley if you desire.

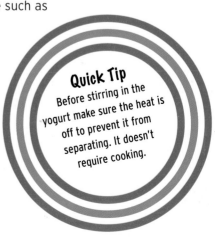

Quick Tip
Before stirring in the yogurt make sure the heat is off to prevent it from separating. It doesn't require cooking.

Variation Rice (see pages 70-71) is an ideal accompaniment for this dish.

Chicken Satay Kebabs

This is a fun way to serve chicken, but make sure there are no peanut allergies in the family before serving to younger children.

Serves 4
20 minutes, plus marinating time

Ingredients

2 chicken breasts, skinned and boned

4 tbsp sunflower oil

2 cloves garlic, crushed

1 tsp caster (superfine) sugar

½ tsp ground cumin

½ tsp ground coriander

1 tbsp light soy sauce

Satay sauce:

8 tbsp smooth peanut butter

8 tbsp hot chicken stock

½ tsp chilli powder

Smart Shopper

The Chinese and Japanese use soy sauce in their cuisine. The Chinese make dark and light soy sauce, with the dark sauce being fermented longer and having a stronger taste, more suitable for adults. The standard Japanese soy sauce (sometimes labelled <u>shoyu</u>) is light compared to Chinese soy sauce. It is also sweeter and less salty.

① Cut each chicken breast lengthways into 8 long strips. Combine the oil, garlic, sugar, spices, and soy sauce in a shallow dish and add the chicken strips. Toss to coat the strips and let marinate for at least 1 hour, up to 12 hours, in the refrigerator.

② Thread the chicken strips onto skewers and cook under a hot grill (broiler) for 6-8 minutes, turning frequently.

③ While the chicken is cooking, combine the peanut butter, stock, and chilli powder to form a smooth sauce.

④ Serve the chicken strips still on the skewers with the peanut sauce.

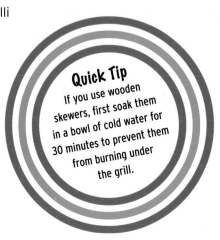
Quick Tip
If you use wooden skewers, first soak them in a bowl of cold water for 30 minutes to prevent them from burning under the grill.

Variation You can add a cored, seeded, and chopped red or green **pepper**. Add before the tomatoes and let simmer for a few minutes.

Chilli con Carne

When served with rice (see pages 70-71), this makes a complete meal that will be truly welcomed on a cold day.

 Serves 4
60 minutes

Ingredients

1 tbsp olive oil

1 onion, chopped

2 red chillies, seeded and chopped

2 cloves garlic, chopped

500g/1lb2oz lean minced beef

400g/14oz can chopped tomatoes

400g/14oz can red kidney beans, drained and rinsed

150ml/5floz/²⁄₃ cups beef stock

2 tbsp tomato purée

Yogurt or soured cream to serve

Fresh herbs to garnish

Smart Shopper

Chillis vary immensely in the amount of heat they produce, from none to extremely intense. Jalapeño peppers are often used when a recipe calls for a chilli pepper. These peppers also vary in heat intensity, and mild ones are now available. When you purchase the peppers, make sure their heat intensity will suit you and your family.

① Heat the olive oil in a saucepan and sauté the onion for 5 minutes until softened. Add the chillies and garlic and cook for another 2 to 3 minutes.

② Add the beef and cook until browned, breaking the meat up as it cooks.

③ Stir in the tomatoes, kidney beans, stock, and tomato purée. Bring to the boil, reduce the heat, and simmer for 30 minutes.

④ Serve with yogurt or soured cream and garnish with fresh herbs.

Chilli Enchiladas

Make the chilli as above. Preheat the oven to 180°C/350°F/gas mark 4. Lightly grease a baking dish. Divide the meat filling between 8 flour or corn tortillas and roll up to enclose the filling. Place in the greased dish.

Pour 300ml/10floz/1¼ cup white sauce (see page 63) over the tortillas and sprinkle 50g/2oz/½ cup grated Cheddar cheese on top. Bake for 20 minutes until the cheese melts and the tortillas are hot.

Quick Tip
Chilli peppers can be very hot. Always wear rubber gloves when chopping them up, and avoid touching your eyes – it will sting!

Variation To make a vegetarian meal, simply replace the sausages with **vegetarian sausages.**

Sausage Casserole

Sausages are always popular with the family. They make a great meal served with some colorful vegetables.

 Serves 4
30 minutes

Ingredients

8 good quality sausages

1 tbsp sunflower oil

1 small onion, cut into wedges

2 courgettes (zucchini), trimmed and thickly sliced

1 red pepper, seeded and cut into chunks

1 yellow pepper, seeded and cut into chunks

225ml/8floz/1 cup pasatta

225ml/8floz/1 cup vegetable stock

10 cherry tomatoes

Smart Shopper

Pasatta is basically ripe uncooked tomatoes that have been puréed and sieved to remove the skin and seeds. It may be either smooth or slightly chunky. It's useful in soups, sauces, pasta dishes, and casseroles. If you can't find it in your store, simply drain some canned tomatoes and push through a sieve to make your own.

① Without adding any oil, fry the sausages in a saucepan until browned on all sides. Remove them from the pan. Pour off any fat from the sausages and wipe out the pan.

② Heat the oil in the pan, add the onions, and cook for 4-5 minutes, until they begin to soften. Add the courgettes (zucchini), peppers, pasatta, and stock. Bring to the boil.

③ Reduce the heat and return the sausages to the pan. Simmer gently for 25 minutes.

④ Add the cherry tomatoes and cook for a further 15 minutes before serving.

Quick Tip
To remove seeds from a pepper, lay it on its side and cut down one side. Turn the pepper and cut down the sides until you reach the other end.

Variation If you don't like prawns (shrimp), you can omit them and replace with some more **white fish**.

Fish Pie

This fish "pie" is topped with mashed potatoes, which makes even children who don't like fish want to try it.

Serves 4
1 hour 45 minutes

Ingredients

6 medium potatoes, peeled and cut into chunks or 1cm/½ inch cubes

450g/1lb white fish fillets such as cod or haddock, skinned

115g/4oz peeled prawns (shrimp)

600ml/20floz/2½ cups milk

6 tbsp butter

2 leeks, washed, trimmed, and sliced

6 tbsp plain (all-purpose) flour

2 hard-boiled eggs

Salt and freshly ground black pepper

Smart Shopper

The best place to buy is from a reputable fish supplier. The fish should always be in a refrigerated case or kept on ice. The fish should have a seawater-like smell, firm flesh, and its surface should be bright and clear – in fact, almost translucent. Pink or brown spots indicate bruising or spoilage. Avoid frozen fish that looks dry and chalky.

1. Place the potatoes in a saucepan and add enough water to just cover them. Bring quickly to the boil and add a little salt. Reduce the heat and simmer for 10-15 minutes until just tender.

2. Meanwhile, preheat the oven to 200°C/400°F/gas mark 6. Place the fish and milk in a saucepan. Cover and when the milk begins to boil, reduce the heat a little and cook for 10 minutes or until the fish flakes easily.

3. Remove the fish with a draining spoon. Strain the milk throughly a sieve and reserve. Break up the fish into large chunks with a fork.

4. When the potatoes are cooked, drain them thorough and return to the heat for a few seconds to remove any remaining moisture. Mash them well.

5. Melt 4 tbsp of butter in a saucepan and add the leeks. Cook gently for 3 minutes or until softened. Stir in the flour and cook for another minute. Gradually stir in the reserved milk and heat, stirring constantly, until the sauce thickens. Season with salt and pepper.

6. Place the fish in an ovenproof dish and arrange the prawns (shrimp) and egg on top. Spoon over the sauce. Spoon the mashed potato on top of the fish. Melt the remaining butter and brush over the top.

7. Bake for 35-45 minutes until the top is crisp and golden.

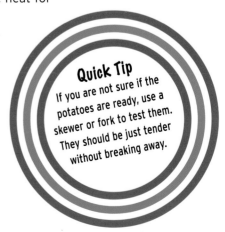

Quick Tip
If you are not sure if the potatoes are ready, use a skewer or fork to test them. They should be just tender without breaking away.

Variation Instead of the soured cream you can serve these salmon cakes with **natural (plain) yogurt** or a **tomato salsa.**

Salmon Fish Cakes

To make the cakes ahead of time, wrap them in clingfilm (plastic wrap), then chill in the refrigerator.

Serves 4
45 minutes

Ingredients

350g/12oz potatoes, peeled and cut into small chunks

400g/14oz canned salmon, drained

2 tbsp mayonnaise

2 tbsp plus 2 tsp freshly chopped dill or parsley

Salt and freshly ground black pepper

50g/2oz/1 cup dried breadcrumbs

Sunflower oil for frying

150ml/5floz/⅔ cup soured cream

Lemon wedges to serve

Fresh dill or parsley to garnish

Smart Shopper

Herbs provide the best flavor when they are fresh. You can use either curly-leaf parsley or flat-leaf (or Italian) parsley. When buying herbs make sure the leaves aren't wilted and don't have yellow or brown spots. In a pinch, you can use a teaspoon crumbled dried leaves for every tablespoon of finely chopped, fresh leaves.

① Cook the potatoes in lightly salted boiling water for 10-15 minutes until just tender.

② Meanwhile, drain the salmon and empty into a mixing bowl. Discard any skin and bones and break up the flesh with a fork.

③ Drain the potatoes well and mash. Add to the fish, then add the mayonnaise and 2 tbsp of the herbs. Season and mix until well combined.

④ Shape the mixture into 8 flattened rounds, then coat in the breadcrumbs. Chill until required.

⑤ Mix the soured cream and the remaining 2 tsp of herbs together, season with salt and pepper, and transfer to a serving dish.

⑥ Heat the oil in a frying pan and shallow fry the salmon cakes for 5-10 minutes until heated through and crisp. Serve with the soured cream and lemon wedges for squeezing. Garnish with fresh herbs.

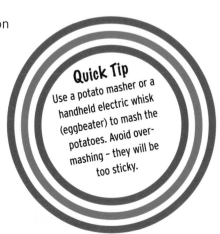
Quick Tip
Use a potato masher or a handheld electric whisk (eggbeater) to mash the potatoes. Avoid over-mashing – they will be too sticky.

Easy Herb Risotto

Making a risotto is simple, and once you master this basic risotto, it can be used as a base for many variations.

Serves 4
45 minutes

Ingredients

2 tbsp olive oil

1 onion, chopped

1 clove garlic, chopped

350g/12oz/1¾ cups risotto rice

150ml/5floz/⅔ cup dry white wine

1 litre/34floz/4¼ cups vegetable or chicken stock

6 tbsp good-quality pesto, preferably homemade

85g/3oz/¾ cup freshly grated Parmesan cheese

Salt and freshly ground black pepper

Lemon wedges to serve

Smart Shopper

The Italians have perfected the art of cooking risotto so that it has a creamy texture but a resilient bite to the grain. Preferably, look for rice imported from Italy, labelled "*superfino*" grade, such as Arborio rice. If you can't find an imported Italian rice, you can substitute with an American short- or medium-grain rice.

① Heat the oil in a saucepan and fry the onion for 4–5 minutes until softened but not colored. Add the garlic and cook for 1 minute. Stir in the rice and cook over a medium-high heat for 1-2 minutes, stirring constantly.

② Add the wine and turn down the heat so that the liquid is gently simmering. Cook, stirring, until the wine has been absorbed.

③ Place the stock in a pan, heat until hot, and keep warm over a low heat. Meanwhile, add a ladleful of stock at a time to the risotto mixture and cook, stirring, until the stock has been absorbed. Repeat until all of the stock has been added and the rice is tender.

④ Stir in the pesto and cheese and season to taste. Serve immediately with lemon wedges for squeezing over the risotto.

☒ **Pea and Ham Risotto**
Use 115g/4oz chopped ham and 115g/4oz/⅔ cup cooked frozen peas in place of the pesto. Add them before the last two ladles of stock.

☒ **Asparagus and Broccoli Risotto**
Use 225g/8oz/1½ cups asparagus cut into short lengths and 115g/4oz/1¼ cups broccoli florets instead of the pesto. Cook in the simmering stock for 3 minutes until just tender; remove and set aside. Add them to the risotto before the last two ladles of stock.

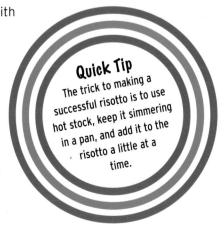
Quick Tip
The trick to making a successful risotto is to use hot stock, keep it simmering in a pan, and add it to the risotto a little at a time.

Variation If your children love carrots, you can add two medium diced **carrots** after the garlic and let cook for 3-4 minutes before stirring in the tomatoes.

Spaghetti & Meatballs

A young child may find spaghetti a bit difficult to say, but it won't matter when it comes to eating this favorite dish.

Serves 4
60 minutes

Ingredients

500g/1lb2oz minced (ground) pork or beef

50g/2oz/1 cup fresh breadcrumbs

1 egg

2 tbsp tomato purée

1 tsp dried mixed herbs

2 tbsp olive oil

1 onion, chopped

1 clove garlic, chopped

500g/1lb2oz pasatta or canned chopped and peeled tomatoes

400g/14oz spaghetti

Grated Parmesan cheese to serve

Smart Shopper

You'll find Parmesan cheese sold in several forms in the supermarket. The most basic, already grated and preserved, will be found on the shelves. Fresh cheese is sold in the refrigerated dairy section, either in solid blocks that you can grate yourself using a fine grater or already grated. Fresh cheese has the best flavor.

① Place the meat, breadcrumbs, egg, tomato purée, and herbs in a mixing bowl and season well with salt and pepper. Mix until well combined, then shape into 18-20 balls. Chill until required.

② Heat 1 tbsp oil in a large frying pan and fry the meatballs in one or two batches until browned all over. Remove from the pan and keep warm. Wipe out the pan and heat the remaining oil, add the onion, and cook over a low heat for 3-4 minutes until softened. Stir in the garlic and cook for 1 minute.

③ Stir in the tomatoes and bring to the boil. Season to taste. Return the meat balls to the pan and reduce the heat so the sauce is gently simmering. Cook for 20-25 minutes, turning the meatballs over occasionally so that they do not stick to the bottom of the pan and burn.

④ Meanwhile, cook the spaghetti in plenty of lightly salted boiling water for 10 minutes or as directed on the packet.

⑤ Drain and divide between four serving plates. Spoon the meat balls and sauce on top and serve sprinkled with Parmesan cheese.

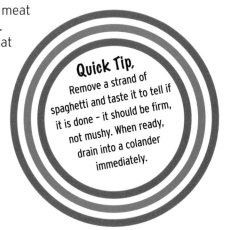

Quick Tip,
Remove a strand of spaghetti and taste it to tell if it is done – it should be firm, not mushy. When ready, drain into a colander immediately.

Variation To add a little color, try adding some **sweet corn niblets** (corn kernels) and fried diced **red pepper** to the pasta before baking it.

Macaroni Cheese

This family favorite is served here with a delicious topping of caramelized onions.

 Serves 4
40 minutes

Ingredients

400g/14oz macaroni or other dried pasta shapes

3 tbsp butter

4 tbsp plain (all-purpose) flour

600ml/20floz/2½ cups milk

115g/4oz/1 cup Cheddar or Moneterey Jack cheese, grated

Pinch of freshly grated nutmeg

2 tbsp olive oil

1 large onion, thinly sliced

1 tsp granulated sugar

Smart Shopper

Pasta comes in many shapes, and some are made in stars and letter shapes to appeal to children. These are too small to use in this dish, so look for ones of similar size to macaroni, such as shell and bow-tie shapes or twirly types. Different shapes will have different cooking times, so always follow the package directions.

① Cook the pasta in plenty of lightly salted boiling water as directed on the package. Preheat the oven to 180°C/350°F/gas mark 4.

② Meanwhile, melt the butter in a saucepan. Stir in the flour and cook for 30 seconds. Remove from the heat and gradually add the milk while stirring.

③ Return the mixture to the heat and cook, stirring until the sauce thickens. Add most of the cheese and stir until melted. Season to taste with salt, pepper, and nutmeg.

④ Drain the cooked pasta, add the sauce to it, and toss together. Put into a shallow ovenproof dish and sprinkle the remaining cheese on top. Bake in the oven for 10 minutes while cooking the onions.

⑤ Heat the oil in a small frying pan with the oil. Add the onions and cook over a low heat, stirring until they begin to color, about 5 minutes. Add the sugar and cook for a few more minutes until golden brown.

⑥ Serve the macaroni cheese with the onions scattered on top.

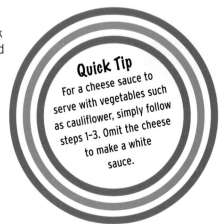

Quick Tip
For a cheese sauce to serve with vegetables such as cauliflower, simply follow steps 1-3. Omit the cheese to make a white sauce.

Variation Experiment with the combination of vegetables - try adding sliced **mushrooms**, diced **red pepper**, and **broccoli** florets.

Chicken on a Stir Fry

Slice up the stir-fried vegetables before you start cooking the grilled chicken for this Chinese-inspired meal.

 Serves 4
30 minutes

Ingredients

3 chicken breasts, skinned and boned

1 tbsp sunflower oil, plus extra for brushing

Ground black pepper

1 small onion, sliced

3 carrots, peeled and cut into matchsticks

150g/5oz/1 cup mangetout (snow peas), trimmed

2 courgettes (zucchini), thinly sliced

85g/3oz/¾ cup bean sprouts

1 tbsp dark soy sauce

1 tbsp Worcestershire sauce

2 tbsp clear honey

1 to 2 tsp chilli sauce

1 tsp corn flour (cornstarch)

Smart Shopper

Mung bean sprouts are the most common type of sprouts used in Chinese cooking, but Asian markets also carry soybean sprouts. These are thicker, with yellow heads, and must be cooked for 1 minute before eating (mung bean sprouts don't require cooking). Don't buy wilting or browning sprouts as these won't be fresh.

① Place the chicken breasts between two sheets of clingfilm (plastic wrap) and flatten slightly with a meat mallet or rolling pin. Brush each side with a little oil and season with ground black pepper.

② Heat a griddle pan or grill to high and cook the chicken for 4–5 minutes each side.

③ Heat the oil in a wok or frying pan and add the onion, carrots, mangetout (snow peas), and courgettes (zucchini), and cook for 5 minutes. Add the sprouts and cook for 1 minute.

④ Mix together the soy sauce, Worcestershire sauce, honey, chilli sauce, and corn flour (cornstarch). Add to the wok and cook, stirring, until the sauce thickens.

⑤ To serve, cut the chicken into three or four pieces, pile the stir-fried vegetables onto the plates, and top with the chicken.

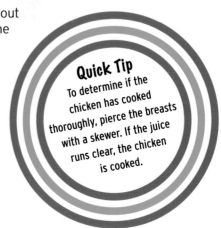

Quick Tip
To determine if the chicken has cooked thoroughly, pierce the breasts with a skewer. If the juice runs clear, the chicken is cooked.

Variation You can serve these chips (fries) with a **tomato relish** or **salsa** as a tasty snack. Or try **mayonnaise**, Dutch style.

Crispy Potato Wedges

These oven baked potato wedges are always popular with children. They have much less fat than deep-fried potatoes.

 Serves 4
30 minutes

Ingredients
6 medium potatoes, scrubbed
2 tbsp olive oil
1 clove garlic, chopped
1 tsp dried thyme or 2 tsp paprika
Sea salt

Smart Shopper
You can find several types of salt in the supermarket: the standard table salt (check the label for additives), which is fine enough to use in a salt shaker; rock salt, often ground in a salt mill; and sea salt. Sea salts are usually unrefined so they contain more trace minerals than other types. Avoid using too much salt for children.

1. Preheat the oven to 200°C/400°F/gas mark 6.
2. Cut the potatoes into wedges.
3. Place the oil, garlic, and thyme or paprika in a mixing bowl. Add the potatoes and toss until well coated with the oil mixture.
4. Spread the wedges out in a single layer on a baking sheet.
5. Bake for 30 minutes until tender. Serve sprinkled with sea salt.

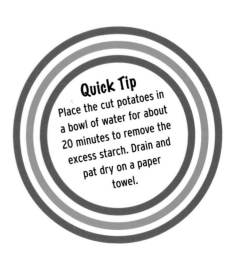

Quick Tip
Place the cut potatoes in a bowl of water for about 20 minutes to remove the excess starch. Drain and pat dry on a paper towel.

Mashed Potatoes

There are many variations to mashed potatoes, but here's a basic one that is sure to please.

 Serves 4
30 minutes

Ingredients
6 medium floury potatoes, peeled
3 tbsp butter
85–125ml/3–4floz/⅓–½ cup milk
Salt and freshly ground black pepper

Smart Shopper
The best mashed potatoes are made with floury potatoes not waxy ones. Varieties of white and yellow potatoes are often the best to choose. New potatoes are not suitable as they have a waxy texture. As with all potatoes, avoid those with green areas on the skin and with wrinkled skin.

① Cut the potatoes into even-sized pieces. Place in a saucepan and add enough water to just cover the potatoes. Bring quickly to the boil; add a little salt. Reduce the heat and simmer for 10-15 minutes, depending on the size of the pieces, until just tender.

② Meanwhile, heat the milk until almost boiling. Add the butter to the milk. Drain the potatoes.

③ Mash the potatoes, using a potato masher, potato ricer, or handheld electric whisk (eggbeater). Add the hot milk, a little at a time, until you reach the desired consistency, beating until well combined. Season with salt and pepper.

Mustard Mash:
Add 2 tbsp whole-grain mustard to the potatoes with the butter and milk.

Garlic Mash:
Melt the butter in a separate pan and add 1 to 2 cloves chopped garlic. Cook gently for 1-2 minutes. Add the milk and complete as above.

Quick Tip
After draining the potatoes, return them to the pan and heat quickly for a few seconds to remove any remaining moisture.

Variation Instead of using the bay leaf, sprinkle some chopped **chives** on top to decorate.

Perfect Rice

Rice is a great accompaniment for many dishes. It has the best flavor if cooked by the absorption method.

 Serves 4
20 minutes

Ingredients
285g/10oz/1½ cups basmati rice
675ml/24floz/3 cups water
½ tsp salt
1 bay leaf (optional)

Smart Shopper
Basmati rice is often used in India and Pakistan and it is also grown in the United States. This aromatic rice swells only lengthwise when cooking so the grains stay dry and separate. You can use other types of rice such as short- or long-grained rice, but make sure you add 1 tsp of oil to the water to keep the grains separate.

① Place the basmati rice in a sieve and rinse under running water until the water runs clear.

② Place in a saucepan with a tight-fitting lid. Add the water; bring to the boil over a high heat.

③ As soon as the water boils, add the salt and bay leaf if using. Stir well. Cover and reduce the heat to very low. Cook for 10 minutes. Do not be tempted to lift the lid to take a look – as long as the pan is over a low heat it will be fine.

④ Turn off the heat and allow to stand for 2 minutes before lifting the lid.

⑤ Transfer to a warm serving dish.

Quick Tip
Before transferring the rice to the serving plate you can fluff it up with a fork to make it look more attractive.

Variation Instead of using the zest and juice from a lemon, try using the zest and juice from ½ an **orange.**

Glazed Carrots

Children and adults alike will love these sweet glazed carrots.

 Serves 4
15 minutes

Ingredients

8-10 medium carrots

2 tbsp butter

2 tbsp light brown sugar

Grated zest and juice of ½ lemon

Fresh thyme to garnish

Smart Shopper

There are a variety of carrots available, and you can choose small types and cook them whole. When choosing carrots, the freshest ones will be sold with the leaves still attached. The flesh should be firm, not springy – which indicates an old carrot – and there should be no cracks. Avoid those with green tinges – they will be bitter.

① Peel and cut the carrots into thick slices.

② Cook in lightly salted boiling water for 8-10 minutes, until just tender.

③ Drain well in a colander.

④ Add the butter, sugar, and lemon juice and zest to the pan, and cook, stirring, until the butter melts and the sugar dissolves.

⑤ Return the carrots to the pan and toss over the heat for 1-2 minutes, until well glazed.

⑥ Serve garnished with fresh thyme.

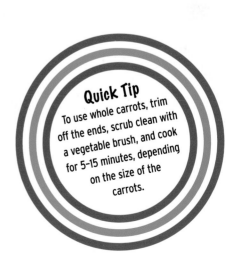

Quick Tip
To use whole carrots, trim off the ends, scrub clean with a vegetable brush, and cook for 5-15 minutes, depending on the size of the carrots.

Variation For a more traditional brownie with nuts, you can replace the peanuts with chopped **walnuts**, or try using chopped **hazelnuts**.

Crunchy Brownies

If you have a child who cannot eat nuts, simply omit them from the recipe – the brownies will still be delicious!

Makes 12
50 minutes

Ingredients

225g/8oz plain (dark) chocolate

225g/8oz/2 sticks butter

3 eggs

115g/4oz/½ cup caster (superfine) sugar

115g/4oz/¾ cup plain (all-purpose) flour

50g/2oz/½ cup cocoa powder

115g/4oz/1 cup unsalted peanuts, chopped

Smart Shopper

When buying peanuts make sure they are unsalted – the salt affects the taste of the brownies. Some nuts, especially peanuts, trigger an allergic reaction, so don't allow a young child to eat them if there is a peanut allergy in a close family member. And keep nuts away from toddlers and other young children who may choke on them.

① Preheat the over to 190°C/375°F/gas mark 5. Grease and line a 25x20cm/10x8 inch cake tin.

② Melt the chocolate and butter in a heatproof bowl balanced over simmering water in a saucepan, or microwave in the oven at 50 percent for 1-2 minutes. Stir until combined.

③ Beat together the eggs and sugar until creamy, then beat in the melted chocolate mixture. Fold in the flour, cocoa powder, and peanuts.

④ Pour into the tin and bake in the oven for 35-40 minutes.

⑤ Cool in the tin and cut into squares to serve.

Quick Tip
If you're not sure if the brownies are baked enough – touch them in the centre – they should be firm. They will harden more as they cool.

Variation Instead of using regular chocolate chips, you can use **white chocolate chips,** or why not use a mixture of the two.

Chocolaty Cookies

These chocolate chip cookies are certain to bring a smile to your children's faces!

 Makes 12-16
30 minutes

Ingredients

150g/5oz/1 stick and 2 tbsp butter, softened

150g/5oz/½ cup and 2 tsp caster (superfine) sugar

1 egg

½ tsp vanilla essence (extract)

200g/7oz/1¾ cup plain (all-purpose) flour

1 tsp baking powder

115g/4oz/1 cup chocolate chips

Smart Shopper

Plain (all-purpose) flour is the most often used flour in the home kitchen and can be used for general baking and storing. Store flour in an air-tight container in a cool cupboard or even in the refrigerator. If you don't plan to use much flour, you can purchase a small bag to avoid having to throw away unused spoiled flour.

1. Preheat the oven to 350°F/180°C/gas mark 4.

2. Beat together the butter and sugar until pale and fluffy with a wooden spoon or handheld electric mixer. Beat in the egg and vanilla essence (extract).

3. Sift the flour and baking powder together, using a sieve over a bowl and shaking until the ingredients fall into the bowl, and beat into the mixture. Add the chocolate chips and stir until well combined.

4. Place spoonfuls of the mixture on a lightly oiled baking sheet, leaving plenty of space around each because the biscuits will spread considerably.

5. Bake for 12-15 minutes until golden. Let cool on the baking sheet for 2-3 minutes, then transfer to a wire rack to cool completely.

Quick Tip

These cookies will keep in an airtight container for 1 week. If you don't want to spoil the kids, freeze some of the batch to eat another time.

Variation Try adding 50g/2oz/½ cup of chopped **walnuts** or ground **almonds** for some extra texture and flavor.

Fruity Crumble

The combination of apples and cherries makes this a nutritious as well as delicious treat.

Serves 4-6
50 minutes

Ingredients

3 medium apples, peeled, cored, and sliced

2 x 400g/14oz can cherry pie filling

For the topping:

50g/2oz/½ cup rolled oats

115g/4oz/1 cup plain (all-purpose) flour

2 tbsp light muscovado (brown) sugar

6 tbsp butter, cut into cubes

Smart Shopper

There are several different types of oats, and these differ in their milling process. Unlike some oats that need more time to cook, rolled oats have been milled to hasten the cooking process, which makes them ideal for baking. Don't try using oats sold to make instant porridge. These will cook too quickly.

① Preheat the oven to 200°C/400°F/gas mark 6.

② Place the apples in a saucepan with 4 tbsp water. Cook over a low heat for 4-5 minutes, until they just begin to soften. Add the cherry filling and stir until well combined.

③ Pour into an ovenproof pie dish (pan).

④ To make the topping, place the oats and flour in a bowl and stir in the sugar. Add the butter and rub in with your fingertips to resemble coarse breadcrumbs. Alternatively, if you have a food processor, place all the ingredients in the bowl and blend until combined.

⑤ Sprinkle the topping over the fruit filling and bake for 25-30 minute or until the top is crisp and golden.

⑥ Serve with yogurt or cream.

Quick Tip
Let the butter stand at room temperature for 10-15 minutes before making the dish to make it softer and easier to break up with your fingers.

Sticky Bananas

These sticky bananas are a great after-meal treat. Serve with a dollop of fresh cream or ice cream.

Serves 4
15 minutes

Ingredients

3-4 bananas

2 tbsp butter

2 tbsp light muscovado (brown) sugar

125ml/4floz/½ cup orange juice

Grated zest and juice of 1 lime

Flaked coconut to serve (optional)

Smart Shopper

The best bananas are plump with vibrant skin. If the skin is dull, the banana won't ripen. Any large black areas indicate bruising - don't buy bruised bananas. Bananas with brown coloring will be too ripe for this recipe, but you can still eat them. Put an underripe banana into a brown paper bag to hasten the ripening process.

① Cut the bananas in half, then cut in half again lengthways. Melt the butter in a heavy-based frying pan, and fry the bananas for 2 minutes, turning once.

② Sprinkle over the sugar and stir in the orange and lime juice. Cook over a low heat until the bananas are soft and the juices are syrupy.

③ Spoon onto serving plates and sprinkle with the coconut, if using, and the lime zest.

Flambé Bananas

For a fabulous adult version of this dish, cook until the juice is syrupy. Then gently heat 4 tbsp rum in a small pan. Carefully set the alcohol alight with a match and pour the flaming rum over the bananas in the pan. Cook until the flames die down and serve.

Quick Tip
You don't need special equipment to extract the juice from the lime. Simply cut it in half and squeeze the juice into a cup - remove any seeds.

Variation Instead of using nuts, you can replace them with **raisins** or chopped **dates**.

Nutty Baked Apples

The basic baked apple has been turned into a real treat with the addition of just a few extra ingredients.

 Serves 4
30 minutes

Ingredients

4 apples

85g/3oz/½ cup cashews

1 tbsp soft brown sugar

½ tsp ground cinnamon

2 tbsp maple syrup

Smart Shopper

Visit the farms and markets during the harvest season in your local area for freshly picked apples. These will have the best flavor and texture. Buy brightly colored, firm apples without bruises or damaged skin. If the flesh gives when pressed, it will be soft. The skin should be taut without signs of shrivelling.

① Preheat the oven to 180°C/350°F/gas mark 4.

② Remove the cores from the apples and score around the girth of the apple with a sharp knife to create a flat bottom that will help the apples stand upright. Place in a shallow baking dish.

③ Coarsely chop the nuts and mix together with the sugar and cinnamon. Use to fill the centre of the apples, pressing down well.

④ Spoon a tablespoon of maple syrup over each apple and bake for 35-45 minutes until soft.

⑤ Serve with yogurt or cream.

Quick Tip

To remove an apple core, insert a corer into the centre of the apple, using even pressure. Twist and remove the core. Or use a small sharp knife.

Variation For a more adult flavor combination, why not try using **coffee** ice cream with **almond macaroon** biscuits.

Dad's Special Sundae

Vary the flavor of ice cream and types of biscuits (cookies) you use according to your family's tastes.

Serves 4
15 minutes

Ingredients

4 scoops of chocolate ice cream

4 scoops of vanilla ice cream

225g/8oz small chocolate chip biscuits (cookies)

Chocolate sauce

Whipped cream

4 glacé cherries or fresh strawberries

Smart Shopper

When buying ice cream from a supermarket make sure the container is not covered with ice crystals – an indication that the ice cream has been exposed to fluctuating temperatures and will have an unappealing coarse, icy texture. Once you buy ice cream, get it home and into the freezer as soon as possible to retain the best qualilty.

① Place a scoop of chocolate ice cream followed by a scoop of vanilla ice cream into four beer mugs or glasses.

② Reserving a few biscuits (cookies) to decorate, break the remaining biscuits into small pieces and pile on top of the ice cream.

③ Spoon a generous layer of chocolate sauce on top of the biscuits and top with dollops of whipped cream.

④ Decorate with the reserved biscuits (cookies) and the cherries or strawberries. Serve immediately.

Quick Tip:
To make it easier to remove ice cream from the container, you can use an ice-cream scoop that has been dipped in hot water.

Tarragon Chicken

Tarragon and garlic make this roast chicken a delicious meal, especially when served with the roasted vegetables.

Serves 4-6
2 hours, depending on size of chicken

Ingredients

1 oven-ready chicken, about 1.4-1.5kg/3-3lb3oz

8 cloves garlic

Few sprigs tarragon

1 lemon

Salt and freshly ground black pepper

1 tbsp plain (all-purpose) flour

300ml/10floz/1¼ cups chicken or vegetable stock

---

① Preheat the oven to 200°C/400°F/gas mark 6. Weigh the chicken and calculate the cooking time. Allow 20 minutes per 450g/1lb plus 20 minutes.

② Rinse the chicken inside and out and pat dry with paper towel. Place the meat in a roasting tin. Place a couple of garlic cloves (no need to peel) inside the chicken and the remaining cloves around the bird. Cut the lemon in half and place half in the cavity with several sprigs of tarragon. Sprinkle the skin with salt and pepper.

③ Cover loosely with foil and roast for 1 hour. Remove the foil and squeeze the juice from the remaining lemon half over the chicken.

④ Continue to cook for the remaining cooking time, basting once or twice. When cooked the juices will run clear when the bird is pierced with a skewer.

⑤ Sprinkle a few tarragon leaves over the bird and cover again with foil. Allow to rest for 15 minutes in a warm place before carving.

⑥ To make gravy, stir the flour into the roasting tin (after removing the chicken and garlic to a warm platter) and cook for a few seconds on the hob (burner) over a low heat. Stir in the stock and cook, stirring, until the gravy thickens.

Roast Potatoes and Parsnips

4 medium potatoes, peeled

2 parsnips, peeled and cut into quarters lengthways and in half again

4 tbsp olive oil

① Preheat the oven to 200°C/400°F/gas mark 6. Parboil (partially cook) potatoes in lightly salted boiling water for 5 minutes, drain, and return to the pan.

② Shake the pan to fluff the sides of the potatoes.

③ Place the oil in a large roasting tin (pan) and heat in the oven for 5 minutes. Add the potatoes to the hot oil and baste.

④ Roast for 15 minutes. Add the parsnips to the tin and baste in the oil. Return to the oven for 45 minutes, basting once or twice with the hot oil, until tender.

Variation Instead of the muffins, serve with **bagels** spread with **cream cheese**, or you can serve with your own choice of toasted **bread**.

Eggs and Salmon

The salmon caviar gives the dish an extra opulence, but it can be omitted if preferred.

 Serves 2
15 minutes

Ingredients

4 eggs

2 tbsp single (light) cream or milk

Freshly ground black pepper

Pinch of grated nutmeg

Knob of butter

2 spring onions (scallions), finely sliced

50g/2oz smoked salmon, cut into thin strips

1 tsp fresh chives, snipped

1 tbsp salmon caviar (optional)

Toasted muffins, bagels, or bread

Smart Shopper

Depending on the type and the smoking process, smoked salmon varies from a pale pink color to reddish brown. The salmon may be sold in large pieces or sliced. Less-expensive trimmings are sometimes available, and these are ideal for this scrambled egg recipe. Follow the label directions for storing in the refrigerator.

① Beat the eggs and cream together and lightly season with the pepper and nutmeg.

② Melt the butter in a small non-stick frying pan and cook the onion for 1 minute until soft.

③ Pour in the egg mixture and using a wooden spoon or spatula, stir the eggs across the bottom of the pan as they start to set to lightly scrambled.

④ When about half the mixture is set, stir in the smoked salmon. Continue to cook, stirring until just set but still creamy.

⑤ Pile onto warm serving plates and sprinkle with salmon caviar and snipped chives.

⑥ Serve with toasted muffins.

Quick Tip
You can buy nutmeg already grated, but for the best flavor purchase a whole nutmeg and grate it yourself using a fine grater.

Variation Instead of the black peppercorns, try **green peppercorns** or you can even use **multicolored peppercorns.**

Steak au Poivre

Serve the steak rare with a simple green salad on the side - dinner doesn't get any easier or more elegant.

Serves 2
15 minutes

Ingredients

2 x 225g/8oz rump, fillet, or sirloin steaks

Pinch of dry mustard powder

1-2 tsp black peppercorns

2 tbsp sunflower oil

Grilled lemon wedges to serve

Smart Shopper

The meat used for a steak - which is basically a slab of meat 2cm/¾ inch up to 7.5cm/3 inches thick - is chosen because it is a naturally tender cut of the meat and can be cooked by a high-heat method such as grilling, broiling, or frying. When choosing a cut, sniff it to make sure it smells fresh.

① Rub the steaks with a little mustard powder. Place the peppercorns in a mortar and crush with a pestle.

② Press the crushed peppercorns onto both sides of the steak.

③ Heat the oil in a heavy-based frying pan, and fry the steaks over a high heat for 3 minutes each side for rare steaks, 4 minutes each side for medium steaks, and 5-6 minutes each side for well-done steaks.

④ Transfer to serving plates and serve with lemon wedges. Crispy Potato Wedges (see pages 66-67) are an ideal accompaniment.

Quick Tip
If you don't have a pestle and mortar in your kitchen, you can purchase coarse black pepper instead of using the peppercorns.

Variation Instead of the green pepper, you can use 8 halved mushrooms.

BBQ Lamb Kebabs

Barbecues can be great fun and make an ideal occasion for family and friends to gather.

 Serves 8
30 minutes, plus marinating time

Ingredients

1kg/2lb4oz lean lamb

1 onion, skin removed

8 tbsp olive oil

Grated zest and juice 1 lemon

2 cloves garlic, crushed

1 tsp dried marjoram

½ tsp dried thyme

2 tbsp freshly chopped parsley

1 red pepper, seeded and cut into chunks

1 green pepper, seeded and cut into chunks

1 yellow pepper, seeded and cut into chunks

1 courgette (zucchini), thickly sliced

Smart Shopper

Look for plump, firm bulbs when buying garlic, and don't buy garlic if it has been sitting in a moist refrigerated section. At home store your garlic in a cool dry place. If the garlic starts to sprout, remove the sprout as it has an unpleasant bitter taste. To remove the sprout, cut the bulb lengthwise and pull out the green shoot.

① Cut the meat into even sized chunks. Grate the onion or chop very finely in a food processor.

② Place the onion on a small plate and place another on top. Over a shallow dish squeeze as much juice as you can from the onion. Stir the oil, lemon zest and juice, garlic, and herbs into the onion juice.

③ Add the meat and toss until well coated in the marinade. Cover and let marinate for at least 2 hours, up to 12 hours, in the refrigerator.

④ Remove the meat from the marinade and thread onto skewers, alternating with the vegetables.

⑤ Cook over hot barbeque coals for 8-12 minutes, turning frequently and basting with any remaining marinade.

Quick Tip:
To crush garlic, whack it with the wide edge of a large knife quickly, then remove the crushed garlic from the split skin.

Variation If you want, you can add a half dozen sliced **mushrooms** to the vegetable mixture instead of the olives, or olive lovers can use both.

Nachos

These make a great snack, whether for the kids, the family together, or grown ups alone.

 Serves 4-6
30 minutes

Ingredients

4 tomatoes

300g/10½oz bag tortilla chips

1 small red pepper, seeded and diced

12 pitted black olives, sliced

2 mild green chillies, sliced

85g/3oz/¾ cup cheese such as mozzarella, Cheddar, or Monterey Jack, grated

Smart Shopper

There is a huge selection of olives available from around the world, including Greece, Italy, Spain, and California. Black olives have been allowed to ripen on the tree longer than green olives before being harvested. Look for unblemished olives without white spots and that are of a uniform color.

① Preheat the oven to 180°C/350°F/gas mark 4.

② Cut the tomatoes in half, scoop out the seeds, and discard. Dice the flesh.

③ Spread half the tortilla chips over the base of an ovenproof dish.

④ Toss together the tomatoes, pepper, olives, and chillies and scatter half the mixture over the tortilla chips.

⑤ Repeat the layers.

⑥ Sprinkle with the grated cheese and place in the oven to warm for 5-10 minutes. The nachos are ready when the cheese has melted.

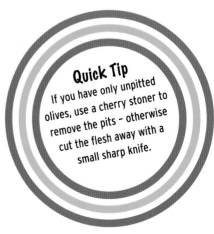

Quick Tip
If you have only unpitted olives, use a cherry stoner to remove the pits – otherwise cut the flesh away with a small sharp knife.

Index